The FITZ

Table of Contents

The Great Lakes' Largest Ship   2

All Hands on Deck   8

The Final Voyage   12

An Unsolved Mystery   18

Raising the Bell   22

Jack Edwards

Rigby

The Great Lakes' Largest Ship

When the *Edmund Fitzgerald* was launched on June 7, 1958, she was the longest vessel to sail the Great Lakes. It took over a year to build this great ship. Thousands came to watch and cheer as the *Edmund Fitzgerald* splashed into the water.

Edmund Fitzgerald, the man, stands in front of *Edmund Fitzgerald*, the ship.

The ship was named after Mr. Edmund Fitzgerald, whose company owned it. His grandfather and his grandfather's five brothers were captains of Great Lakes sailing ships. The many men who sailed this ship nicknamed her the Big Fitz.

The Big Fitz was more than 729 feet long and 75 feet wide. That's longer than two football fields placed end to end!

Her tall yellow striped smokestack was easy to spot from a distance. The hull and deck of the Big Fitz were painted deep shades of red to match the color of the iron ore she carried.

THE BIG FITZ = 729 feet

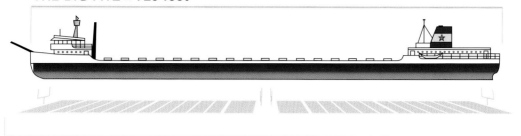

TWO FOOTBALL FIELDS = 720 feet

The Big Fitz was an ore carrier that set many records. Over 26,000 tons of iron ore could be placed in her cargo holds. That's enough ore to make steel for 7,500 automobiles!

pilothouse

bow

EDM

hull

It would take more than 1,000 dump trucks to carry as much iron ore as the Big Fitz carried in a single trip.

The Big Fitz had three cargo holds with 21 covers. The cargo holds were located in the hull of the ship. The covers kept the cargo in and the water out.

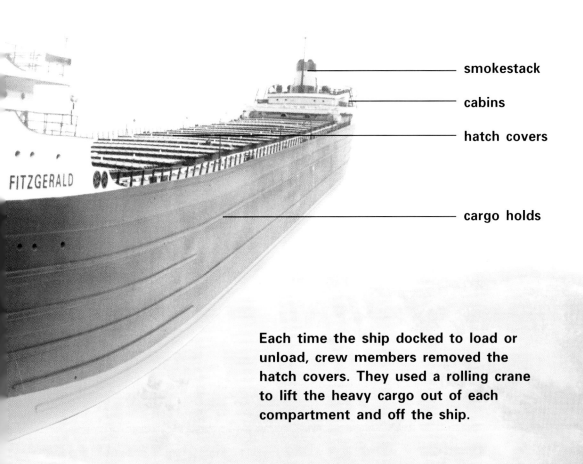

smokestack

cabins

hatch covers

cargo holds

Each time the ship docked to load or unload, crew members removed the hatch covers. They used a rolling crane to lift the heavy cargo out of each compartment and off the ship.

All Hands on Deck

The Big Fitz operated 24 hours a day. Twenty-nine men worked on the ship, and they were divided into shifts. Some worked during the day, while others slept.

In the winter the Great Lakes are covered by large chunks of ice and snow.

The ship was the crew's home for eight months each year. In the winter, when the Great Lakes were frozen over, the crew had four months of vacation.

Everyone ate well and worked hard on the ship. Cooks prepared the meals, and there were always tasks to be done on board, like painting the ship and repairing equipment. In their free time, the crew watched TV, played games, read books, or wrote letters home.

A trip on the Big Fitz began at the loading docks in Superior, Wisconsin. It took about four hours to fill the cargo holds with iron ore pellets that were the size of marbles.

With her cargo holds full, the Big Fitz headed east across Lake Superior to ports where steel was manufactured. These steel mill towns were located along the shore in Illinois, Indiana, Michigan, and Ohio. A round trip took about five days.

Before the Big Fitz returned to Wisconsin, water was pumped into big tanks called ballast tanks. The water in the ballast tanks weighed the ship down when the cargo holds were empty. Without the ballast water, most of the ship's hull would have been out of the water. Wind blowing from either side would have made it hard to steer. Once the crew arrived back in Wisconsin, the ballast water was pumped out, and the cargo holds were filled with iron ore pellets again.

The Final Voyage

On November 9, 1975, the Big Fitz began another routine voyage. The ship was carrying a load of 26,116 tons of iron ore to Detroit, Michigan. That evening, a fierce storm hit the Great Lakes.

With over 30 years of sailing experience on the Great Lakes, Captain Ernest McSorley had sailed through many storms. He thought the bad weather would only delay their arrival.

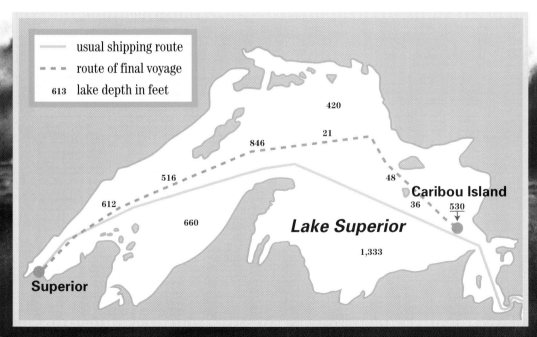

usual shipping route
route of final voyage
613 lake depth in feet

420

21

846

516

48

Caribou Island

612

36   530

660

Lake Superior

1,333

Superior

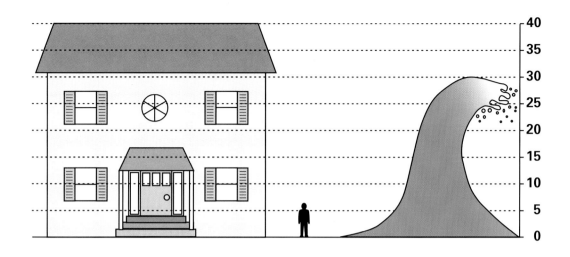

But the storm grew stronger. Powerful winds ranged from 60 to 100 miles an hour, and 30-foot waves crashed over the *Edmund Fitzgerald's* decks.

The storm grew worse. Hail and snow made it hard for the crew to see. Captain McSorley sent a radio message to another cargo ship caught in the storm. He told them the *Edmund Fitzgerald* was taking on water and was listing.

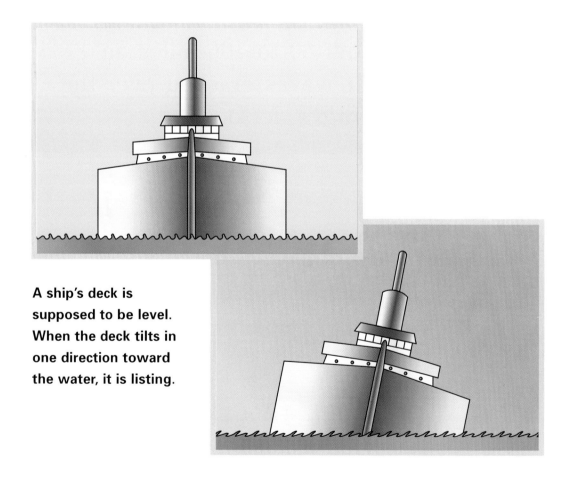

A ship's deck is supposed to be level. When the deck tilts in one direction toward the water, it is listing.

The Coast Guard uses radar screens like these above to map the location of any ships in the area and to watch the route they are traveling.

Later that evening, the captain of the other ship radioed back and asked how the Big Fitz was doing. Captain McSorley replied, "We are holding our own." That was the last message heard from the *Edmund Fitzgerald*. After that, the Big Fitz vanished from radar screens.

A Coast Guard helicopter in action

Within hours, the Coast Guard sent helicopters and planes to search for the *Edmund Fitzgerald*. Other ships joined the search. Friends and family members anxiously waited for news about their loved ones. But no good news came.

The next day, newspapers from all over the United States ran headlines about the disaster that took place on Lake Superior.

CLOUDY
cloudy, chance of show-
uesday, High 60s. Low
nd 30s. Maps and tables
- Page 11 of Part 2.

PAGES—2 PARTS

MILWAUKEE SENTINEL

TUESDAY MORNING, NOVEMBER 11, 1975

★ ★ ★ ★ ★ FINAL

30 to 35 Aboard on Lake Superior

SHIP FEARED LOST IN STORM

Hikes

Fitzgerald Owned by

$114

By AVI LANK

Increases in pay ar
benefits for Milwau
county and School T
ployes in 1975 and
amount to a total
$114.3 million, acc
figures gathered an
by The Milwaukee S

If the entire sum
through the prope
increases would
equivalent of $402
es over a two-ye

Weather
Showers
Details on Page 5A

The Detroit News

AMERICA'S LARGEST EVENING CIRCULATION

163rd YEAR NO. 81

TUESDAY, NOVEMBER 11, 1975

Finance
Pages 2D to 5D
Races
Page 4E

15

Freighter sinks; crew of 29

Zion is hunted ke Superior

WAUKEE JOURNAL

Latest Edition††

Tuesday, November 11, 1975— ©1975, The Milwaukee Journal

The Edmund Fitzgerald, shown in a file photograph, disappeared in a storm on Lake Superior Monday

—AP Wirephoto

Search Finds Ship Debris
but No Sign of 29 Men

and perils UN

S. against
re feared

An Unsolved Mystery

All 29 crew members lost their lives in the storm. It was one of the Great Lakes' worst maritime disasters. Fourteen years later, the *Edmund Fitzgerald* made headlines again. An expedition was organized to solve the mystery of the ship's sinking. A robot camera located the wreck 530 feet beneath the cold Lake Superior waters.

The robot could see the pilothouse and the ship's 195-pound bell. The bow was right side up in the water, but the stern was upside down. All that was left of the middle section were twisted pieces of steel. Iron ore pellets had spilled out on the bottom of the lake.

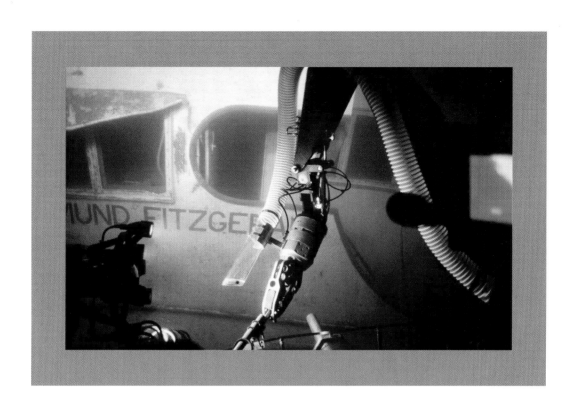

Underwater photos of the sunken ship

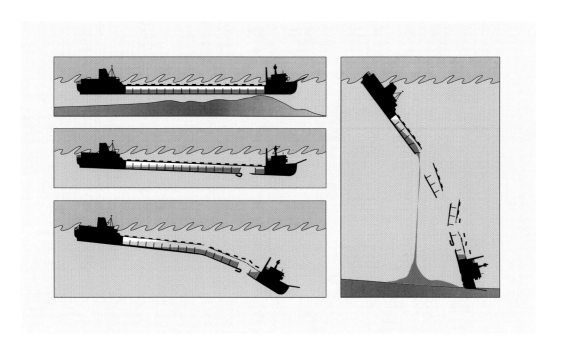

There are many guesses about why the Big Fitz sank. Some people think she hit shallow ground near Caribou Island on Lake Superior. Maybe this ripped a hole in the bottom of the hull. The water pouring into the cargo holds might have made the ship too heavy to stay afloat.

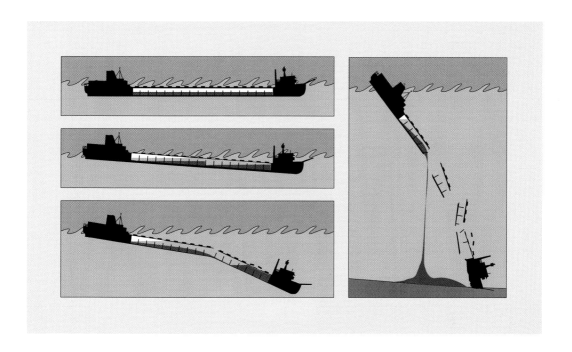

Others think that high waves leaked into the cargo holds around the hatch covers. Then big waves crashing from behind could have pushed one end of the ship up out of the water, causing the water and iron ore in the cargo holds to shift forward. This pushed the other end down below into the water.

We will never know what actually caused the Big Fitz to sink. However, we do know the ship went down quickly. No one had time to call for help. It took over a year to build the Big Fitz, but only seconds for a Lake Superior storm to destroy her.

Raising the Bell

Almost 20 years after the sinking of the *Edmund Fitzgerald*, family members requested an expedition to recover the ship's bell. "Now is our turn to make one last dive to recover the bell. The bell will serve as a memorial, a place to lay flowers and feel close," said Ruth Hudson, mother of one of the lost sailors.

In the summer of 1995, divers cut the *Edmund Fitzgerald's* bell off the top of the pilothouse. In its place, they left a replica of the bell, engraved with the names of the 29 crew members.

Diver Bruce Fuoco wore a special suit called a NEWT-SUIT to brave the cold Lake Superior waters.

D FITZGERALD
REW MEMBERS

..an H. McCarthy   James ..Prat..
..rst Mate   Second Mate

..ll   Edward ..Bindon   Thomas E Edwards
..er   First Ass. Engineer   Second Ass. Engineer

..ampeau   Frederick J. Beetcher   Thomas Bentsen
..er   Porter   Oiler

..ch   Ransom E. Cundy   Bruce L. Hudson
              Watchman   Deckhand

        Joseph W. Mazes   Eugene W. O'Brien
     Special Maintenance Man   Wheelsman

..bert C. Rafferty   Paul M. Riippa   John D. Simmons
..eward   Deckhand   Wheelsman

..h C. Walton   David E. Weiss   Blaine H. Wilh..
                   Cadet (Deck)   Oiler

23

Today, you can see the original bell at the Great Lakes Shipwreck Museum at Whitefish Point, Michigan. Seventeen miles away, the Big Fitz rests peacefully at the bottom of Lake Superior.